Kittentalk

A division of Hodder Headline Limited

© Hodder Children's Books 2005
Published in Great Britain in 2005
by Hodder Children's Books
Text © Claire Bessant
Illustrations © Jennifer Graham
Design by Andrew Summers
Cover design: Hodder Children's Books

The right of Claire Bessant to be identified as the author of the work
has been asserted by him in accordance with the Copyright, Designs
and Patents Act 1988.

10 9 8 7 6 5 4 3 2 1

A catalogue record for this book is available from the British Library

ISBN: 0 340 89376 1

Printed by Bookmarque Ltd, Croydon, Surrey

The paper and board used in this paperback by Hodder Children's
Books are natural recyclable products made from wood grown in
sustainable forests. The manufacturing processes conform to the
environmental regulations of the country of origin.

Hodder Children's Books
a division of Hodder Headline Limited
338 Euston Road
London NW1 3BH

Kittentalk

50 Ways To Make Friends With Your Kitten

Claire Bessant

h

A division of Hodder Headline Limited

What would your kitten have at the top of his Christmas list? Yes, you're right, a cardboard box. Cardboard boxes are the number 1 Kitten Favourite Thing. Make him a kitten 'village' with all sorts of boxes, cut out some holes so he can climb through them as well as in and out, and you will make his day.

Learn to knit together. It's not as easy as it looks, but you can always blame dropped stitches on your kitten's 'help'. Wool is Kitten Favourite Thing number 2 (after cardboard boxes). Give your kitten a little ball of spare wool to play with while you're knitting, and make your knitting into a small 'mouse' toy - she won't mind what shape it is.

Persuade your dad that he needs a new toothbrush - the old one is probably looking rather squashy and certainly won't be cleaning his teeth properly. Coax the kitten on to your lap and gently brush his head with the old soft toothbrush. It will feel just like his mum grooming him with her rough tongue. He will probably purr and fall asleep.

At last, a use for all those boring
newspapers grown-ups leave around
on a Sunday. Build tunnels and paper
tents for your kitten to run through
by standing them in an upside-down
'v' shape on the floor. Best to make
sure that your mum and dad have
read them first though!

Teach your kitten a signal for 'grub's up'. Tap her metal dish, shake a pack of dry catfood or call her name in a sing-song sort of way as you put out her food. Give her a treat if you use this special voice to call her at any other time too. In this way, she's always sure to take an interest in coming when you call her - she might just get another treat.

Go butterfly watching with your
kitten in the summer. A buddleia
bush in the garden is a great place
to start on a sunny day. Take a
blanket to sit on, some kitten treats
and a butterfly spotters' book.
Tick off the different butterflies you
see while he leaps around trying to
catch them.

Let your kitten help with your art project. Kittens can't resist grabbing the top of a wiggling pencil as you draw. They can certainly help you to be creative. Remember not to suck the top of the pencil afterwards though!

Watch out for that Christmas tree!
It's a kitten's idea of an adventure
playground. Best not to put on the
best glass decorations this year.
Make paper ones which won't break
and won't hurt if the kitten pulls
them off. Put something heavy at
the base of the tree so it doesn't fall
over if the kitten goes climbing. Next
year she won't be so interested.

Where is that kitten? In the snuggliest place of course - that tiny space between all the Beanie Babies, teddies and other cuddly toys on your bed - perfect camouflage!

What is the tiniest noise your kitten
can hear? Wait until he is sitting
quietly and then make the smallest
scraping noise you can - like a nail
on a stone. The higher pitched the
noise the better. Watch his ears prick
up and he'll turn around to see
where the sound came from. This is
how cats find their prey. They hear
it, follow the sound and then stalk it
before pouncing.

Is there a kitten tooth fairy? Like children, kittens lose their baby or milk teeth before they grow their larger adult teeth. So don't be upset if you find a tiny tooth around the house - it belongs to your kitten, but it will soon be replaced.

Here's Kitten Favourite Thing number 3 - kitten football. Roll up bits of paper into balls - they don't have to be very big. Choose a shiny floor rather than a carpet if you can, as the paper will slide across it much more easily. Your kitten will dash after it and use her paws to tap the paper ball - you may be surprised how good her dribbling skills are.

Is your kitten right-pawed or left-pawed? Many cats, like people, use one side more than the other. Play different games and make a note of which paw your kitten uses most. Your friends will be amazed when you tell them.

Curious kittens will try nibbling anything. Be careful with plants and flowers in the house, as some can be poisonous. Best to keep them out of the way until the kitten grows up a bit. Once they are older, cats are very sensible about what they eat but, like you when you were small, your kitten might try to eat anything!

Don't be tempted to share your fruit lolly with your kitten - he won't be interested. Cats don't taste sweetness in the way we do. They much prefer the smell and taste of meat or creamy, milky things. In the wild, cats would not naturally find sweet things to eat. They also have to eat meat and cannot be vegetarians.

Although your kitten may love drinking the milk you left in your cornflake bowl, it may upset her tummy. Don't give her ordinary milk - you can buy special kitten milk, which she can enjoy without messy consequences!

Kittens and cats are brilliant watchers. They will sit on the window sill hardly moving and stare out of the window. It's not easy to sit so still - try watching with your kitten and see how long you can stay there without moving. Make a list of all the things you see going on outside.

Learn to kitten watch. Observe your pet very carefully and guess when something catches his attention by watching his body language. He will give you clues by twitching his ears or suddenly looking alert. Listen to the noises which catch his attention and the movements which make him sit up and take notice.

Oops! Good job it wasn't mum's best vase! Time to put precious ornaments away before your kitten gets into real trouble. Your baby brother may not be able to reach the ornaments on the shelf, but the kitten can! She will be very curious and will be able to climb and explore even in high-up places.

Make a kitten scrapbook and record
the details of your kitten's life. Write
about his brother or sisters, how old
he is, when he has his vaccinations at
the vet's, what he eats and how you
play with him. Put in photographs of
him as he grows, with the date
written on the back - you'll be
amazed how quickly he gets bigger.

Keep a record of your kitten's weight as she grows. To begin with, when she is very little, you might be able to use the kitchen scales (remember to wash them afterwards). As she gets bigger, you can weigh yourself on the bathroom scales, weigh yourself holding the kitten and then subtract the smaller number from the bigger number to work out the kitten's weight.

If you have a baby brother or sister you will know that they need to sleep a lot - small kittens are the same. They play lots and then need a cosy place to rest. You can make a comfortable bed from a cardboard box with old soft jumpers or blankets inside which your kitten will enjoy snuggling into. You may have to be patient and wait until he wakes up before you can play together again.

Sometimes it can be difficult to find
your kitten when she decides she
needs a rest - here are some places
to try: among the cuddly toys on
the bed, in the dog's bed, in the
airing cupboard, on the pile of
clean ironing, in the square of sun
on the window sill, in a little box
(the tighter the squeeze the better!),
and in the open drawer of your
clothes' chest.

In his search for cosy places, your kitten may get himself into danger. You need to be on alert so he does not get hurt. Make sure the doors of the tumble drier and the washing machine are kept shut and instruct mum to check every time she uses them - just in case he has climbed in for a warm, quiet nap.

Watch your kitten wash her face. She will lick her paw and rub it over her face, behind her head and over her ears. Even young kittens keep themselves very clean - try washing your face in the same way. A kitten's tongue is rough so that it can comb its fur thoroughly - the closest we can come is a rough flannel for our skin and a comb for our hair.

Think about what your kitten sees.
Get down to his level - the world is a
very different place near the ground.
It will help you to understand how
he sees the world and what can be
frightening when you are that small.
There are a lot of large feet, chair
legs and school bags!

Did you know that blinking your eyes is a friendly sign for cats? When cats are being unfriendly and trying to start a fight, they will stare at each other without blinking. You want your kitten to think you are a friend, so look at your kitten and blink as you talk to her - see if she blinks back.

When your kitten goes to the vet's
for his vaccinations, put one of your
old jumpers in the cat basket for him
to travel with. He will feel better
having your smell there with him
when he goes to a strange place.

If your kitten is just too rough when you play with him and scratches you with his claws, try using one of those fishing rod games which has a pole with a piece of string and the toy attached to the end. The kitten can grab and jump at the toy without getting too close to you.

See if you can find some ping pong
balls. It doesn't matter if they are
old or a bit dented. Ping pong balls
are light and move quickly - ideal for
kitten games. You won't need table
tennis bats!

Do you like privacy in the bathroom?
Your kitten may be the same. Avoid
grabbing her or annoying her when
she is using her litter tray. Otherwise
she may decide it is safer to go to
the toilet under the bed where she
can't be disturbed - and mum might
ask you to clear it up!

Sit quietly and brush your kitten. At the same time you can inspect his coat. Kittens can get fleas - a bit like kids at school getting lice and nits. It can easily be sorted out with medicine from your vet - in fact a lot more easily than sorting out nits!

You have to be very clever to learn what your kitten is trying to tell you when she says meow. Sometimes it is because she wants something - the Hungry Meow. Sometimes it is because she is upset - the Worried Meow. Sometimes she feels alone - the 'I'm Lost' Meow. Later, when she is bigger and catches her first worm or butterfly you might hear the 'Look What I've Got' Meow.

The more you talk to your kitten
and respond to him when you hear
one of his meows, the more likely he
is to keep talking to you and to talk
back to you when you speak to him.
While you are learning from him, he
is training you too!

Careful! You may be used to taking a run and jump on to the settee before watching TV - but your kitten could be snoozing happily under a cushion. Make sure she is safely asleep or playing elsewhere, or just stop jumping - mum will probably be pleased that the poor old settee might last a bit longer too.

Wow! That kitten is crazy! Ever felt full of beans and wanted to charge around the house, over the beds and in and out of all the rooms? Kittens sometimes feel the same way, and they actually do it - it is known as a 'mad half hour'. Stay out of the way and watch, making sure your kitten doesn't get into danger. She'll soon calm down and probably need a sleep, but it is fun to watch.

See what your kitten can do with his front paws compared to what a dog can do with his. Cats' paws are almost like hands. Cats can be very delicate and will gently pat something they find interesting - they may even pat you. They can turn their paws around and even pick things up. Dogs' paws are not so flexible.

Pads underneath the kitten's paws
are very sensitive and will be very
pink and soft. Some cats don't like
you to touch them, perhaps because
it feels like it does when someone
tickles your feet. The pads stay quite
soft even as the cat grows older -
compare them with a dog's pads,
which are rough and hard.

Have you seen your kitten's crab walk? Sometimes, when something frightens him or takes him by surprise, he will walk away while still keeping a close eye on whatever has caused the problem, just in case it comes closer. In this way, he ends up walking sideways, just like a crab.

Kittens react very quickly and do not hide their emotions. If something frightens them, they may fluff up their hair along their body and tail - it happens almost instantly. Look and see what has caused the upset - it may have been next door's dog in the garden or one of your friends running up to the kitten too quickly. She will settle down just as quickly when you reassure her that everything is all right.

How do you tell that your kitten is pleased to see you? He will probably greet you the way he would his cat mum - he will run up to you with his tail up straight and he might purr and rub against your legs. He might even make that 'Hello' meow.

If your kitten starts to wear a collar when she is four or five months old remember to check that it does not get too tight. Get your mum to check that she can put one finger under the collar when it is done up so there is room for the kitten to grow - she will get bigger very quickly.

Kittens are so cuddly and tickleable!
Some will enjoy having a tummy
tickle while others may not. Some
might even get rather cross if you
try to touch them on the tummy, so
find out carefully and slowly what
your kitten wants. You will probably
find she much prefers to be tickled
under her chin.

If your kitten is going to do something you think might be dangerous, how do you get his attention? Try making a quick hissing noise by saying 'ssssssss' very quickly with your teeth together. Cats use a hissing sound when they want to make others take notice. Don't do it all the time or your kitten will get used to it - just keep it for when you want to stop him getting into danger.

Where did it go? Young kittens often enjoy watching the movement of football or even snooker on the television. They watch the ball moving across the screen and then look around the back of the TV to see where it has gone. They soon find out there is nothing behind the TV and lose interest, but it is fun to watch them learning.

A happy dog is a tailwagging dog. Not so a kitten or cat. In the cat world, moving a tail back and forward can mean that the cat is rather angry or confused and it is best to leave him alone until he has settled down. If he is agitated, he may scratch if you try to play with him or pick him up. Never pull his tail.

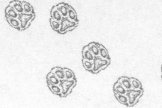

Where did that go? Some games can be very confusing for kittens – bubbles which sail past and then pop, a torch light which moves across the ground but you can't get hold of! Probably rather frustrating but good exercise too.

Ever been picked up by someone you thought was going to drop you? It is quite scary. Learn to pick up your kitten properly so that she can trust you not to drop her. Scoop her up gently by putting one hand under her tummy and the other under her bottom so that she feels safe and secure.

When your kitten is old enough to go outside and has had all his injections at the vet's, you can teach him to use a cat flap. Prop it open and coax him through with his favourite treat. Be patient - he will soon get the idea. If you lock him in at night, you can stick a piece of paper over the flap to let him know that he cannot get through.

When she first goes out, your kitten
may not like the wet grass. She may
try to flick off the water by picking
up each foot and shaking it before
putting it down again. It is very funny
to watch. Of course she will soon get
used to rain and dew, but to begin
with it will be rather strange.

You and your kitten can be great
friends. Try to understand him and
treat him with care and he will be
delighted to play with you and stay
with you.